MW01141835

Party Food

Sharon Dalgleish

Smart Apple Media

This edition first published in 2006 in the United States of America by Smart Apple Media.

Smart Apple Media
2140 Howard Drive West
North Mankato
Minnesota 56003

First published in 2006 by
MACMILLAN EDUCATION AUSTRALIA PTY LTD
627 Chapel Street, South Yarra, Australia 3141

Visit our Web site at www.macmillan.com.au

Associated companies and representatives throughout the world.

Library of Congress Cataloging-in-Publication Data

Dalgleish, Sharon.
    Party food / by Sharon Dalgleish.
      p. cm. — (Healthy choices)
    Includes index.
    ISBN-13: 978-1-58340-746-2
    1. Nutrition—Juvenile literature. 2. Cookery—Juvenile literature. 3. Entertaining—Juvenile literature. I. Title.

RA784.D342 2006
641.5'637—dc22

                                                        2005056807

Edited by Helen Bethune Moore
Text and cover design by Christine Deering
Page layout by Domenic Lauricella
Photo research by Legend Images
Illustrations by Paul Konye

Printed in USA

Acknowledgments
The author and the publisher are grateful to the following for permission to reproduce copyright material:

Front cover: Birthday party, courtesy of Corbis Royalty Free.

Brand X Pictures, pp. 21 (left & centre), 26 (left); Corbis Digital Stock, p. 10 (bottom); Rob Cruse, pp. 6, 21 (right); Digital Vision, p. 9 (top right); iStockphoto.com, p. 4 (left), 8; MEA Photo, pp. 13 (top), 29 (left); Photodisc, pp. 7, 9 (bottom right), 10 (top), 26 (right), 27 (both); Photolibrary/Foodpix, p. 20 (top left & bottom); Photolibrary/Plainpicture Gmbh & Co. Kg, pp. 4 (centre), 30; Photolibrary/Reso E.E.I.G, p. 4 (right); Photos.com, pp. 9 (left), 11; Sarah Saunders, pp. 1, 3, 12, 13 (centre & bottom), 20 (top right), 25, 28, 29 (right).

While every care has been taken to trace and acknowledge copyright, the publisher tenders their apologies for any accidental infringement where copyright has proved untraceable. Where the attempt has been unsuccessful, the publisher welcomes information that would redress the situation.

Contents

Healthy, fit, and happy 4

Why make healthy choices? 6

Snacks 8
Make party dip 10
Make healthy dippers 11

Fun food 12
Make sausage rolls 14
Make chicken nuggets 16
Make party pizza 18

Sweet treats 20
Make fruit sticks 21
Make an ice cream birthday cake 22

Drinks 24
Make party punch 26
Make ice-block surprises 27

Party bags 28

Healthy choices for life 30

Glossary 31

Index 32

Healthy, fit, and happy

To be healthy, fit, and happy your body needs:

- a good mix of foods
- plenty of clean drinking water
- a **balance** of activity and rest

water

activity

A good mix of foods, water, rest, and play all help to make you healthy.

mix of foods

Party food

We all like fun party food. The food group pyramid can help you make party choices that are fun and healthy.

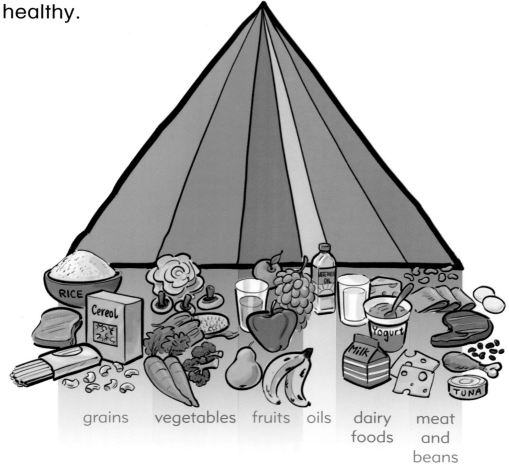

grains   vegetables   fruits   oils   dairy foods   meat and beans

The food group pyramid shows you which foods to eat most for a healthy, balanced diet.

Why make healthy choices?

Making healthy party choices is important. It is fine to eat **sugary** or fatty treats once in a while. However, too much unhealthy food is bad for your body.

Add chocolate chips to nuts and dried fruit mix and you will have a healthy party mix!

Plan an action-packed party. You could have a mini-Olympics in the backyard or at a park.

Active party games keep the focus on fun and are good for your body.

Snacks

Have a few bowls of tasty snacks ready for party guests when they arrive. Your guests can eat snacks with their fingers.

Popcorn is a healthier choice than chips.

Fruit and cheese looks special cut up and arranged nicely on a plate. Avoid using apples and bananas as they turn brown after they are cut.

Here are some ideas for delicious party food you could serve.

Make a party dip

Have a plate of colorful vegetable sticks ready to serve with this dip. Try carrot, cucumber, zucchini, celery, or any of your favorite vegetables.

Serves 2 to 3

What you need
- 1 avocado, halved
- 2 tablespoons lemon or lime juice
- vegetables, cut into sticks
- a spoon
- a mixing bowl
- a fork

What to do
1 **Dig out the seed of the avocado with a spoon.**
2 **Spoon the avocado into a bowl and mash it with a fork.**
3 **Add the lime or lemon juice.**
4 **Mix well and serve with vegetable sticks.**

Lemon or lime juice added to mashed avocado will keep it looking fresh.

Make healthy dippers

Ask a parent or teacher for help.

You could serve the party dip with these healthy dippers.

Allow 1 bread slice per serve

What you need
- bread slices (crusts removed) or pita bread
- a knife
- a baking tray
- oven heated to 300 °F (150 °C)

What to do

1 **Ask an adult to cut the bread into small triangles.**

2 **Arrange in a single layer on a baking tray.**

3 **Bake in oven until triangles are crunchy.**

4 **Serve with party dip.**

Pita bread can be cut into long, thin triangles.

Fun food

Make sure your party food is fun and different from things you eat every day. Serving a healthy main course will give your party guests lots of **energy**.

Use cookie cutters to turn everyday sandwiches into party sandwiches.

One way to make party food exciting is to plan it around a theme or main idea. You could have a spooky party and call the food spooky names.

baked cockroaches
(dates)

fingers of mashed ghost
with mouse droppings
(cream cheese and raisin
sandwiches)

rolled brains dipped in blood
(sausage rolls with ketchup)

**Make your guests laugh by
giving the food funny names.**

13

Make sausage rolls

Homemade sausage rolls will make your hungry party guests happy. Check first that your guests like to eat meat.

Serves 6

What you need

- 10 ounces (300 grams) sausage meat
- ¼ cup tomato paste
- 1 egg
- ½ cup dry breadcrumbs
- 2 sheets ready-rolled puff pastry
- a small bowl of milk
- a large mixing bowl
- a baking tray
- a knife
- a pastry brush
- oven heated to 400 °F (200 °C)

What to do

1 Put the sausage meat, tomato paste, egg and breadcrumbs in the bowl. Mix well. Divide the mixture into four.

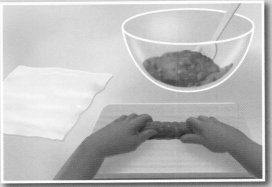

2 Cut the pastry sheets in half. Shape each quarter of the mixture into a sausage as long as the pastry.

Ask a parent or teacher for help.

3 Place sausage mixture in the middle of each piece of pastry. Roll pastry over to cover the sausage mix.

4 Cut each long roll into four. Place the small rolls on the baking tray. Brush the tops with a little milk. Bake for about 15 minutes until golden.

Make chicken nuggets

These nuggets are healthier than most because they are not fried in oil. Check first that your guests like to eat meat.

Serves 6

What you need

- 1¾ cups dry breadcrumbs
- ¼ cup finely grated Parmesan cheese
- 1 egg
- ¼ cup low-fat milk

- 17 ounces (500 grams) chicken breast with no bones or skin
- 2 mixing bowls
- a baking tray
- oven heated to 400 °F (210 °C)

What to do

1 **Put the breadcrumbs and cheese in a bowl. In another bowl, lightly beat the egg and milk.**

2 **Cut the chicken into about 16 chunks. Dip each chunk into the milk mixture.**

Ask a parent or teacher for help.

3 Then dip each chunk into the crumb mixture. Press the crumb mixture firmly onto each nugget.

4 Place the nuggets in a single layer on the baking tray. Bake for about 5 minutes on each side until golden and cooked through.

Make party pizza

You could have a healthy pizza party. You could even let your guests make their own pizzas.

What you need

- 1 mini pizza crust for each person
- pizza sauce
- grated cheese
- red, green, or yellow peppers, sliced
- tomato, sliced

- mushroom, sliced
- ham, sliced
- pineapple pieces
- avocado, sliced
- oven heated to 400 °F (210 °C)
- a baking tray

What to do

1 **Place the mini pizza crusts on a baking tray and bake for 5 minutes.**

2 **Cool a little, and then spread pizza sauce evenly on the bread.**

3 **Sprinkle with cheese and add your favorite toppings.**

4 **Bake for 8 to 9 minutes. Let the pizza cool a little before eating.**

Sweet treats

Try not to eat too many sugary sweets because they have very few **nutrients**. Make tasty, healthy, and sweet treats instead. Your guests will still love them.

Chunks of pineapple rolled in coconut

Fruit Jell-O with real juice

Strawberries dipped in melted chocolate

Make fruit sticks

Ask a parent or teacher for help.

You can make these fruit sticks before the party, or let your guests thread their own.

Serves 8

What you need
- 2 bananas, sliced thickly
- 4 kiwis, chopped into wedges
- 1 container of strawberries
- 1 tablespoon lemon juice
- 8 bamboo sticks
- 1 cup dark chocolate chips, melted

What to do
1 Dip banana slices in lemon juice so they do not go brown.
2 Thread fruit onto sticks.
3 Drizzle melted chocolate over the top.
4 Store in fridge if you have made them before the party.

Make an ice cream birthday cake

An ice cream cake is fun, and healthier for you than a cake with lots of sugary icing.

Serves 8

What you need

- 1¾ pints (1 liter) vanilla ice cream, softened
- 1 container of strawberries, washed and sliced
- a large bowl
- tin foil
- a cake tin
- a plate that will fit in freezer
- extra fruit, flowers, or candles

What to do

1 **Tip softened ice cream into a large bowl. Gently mix in strawberries.**

2 **Line a round cake tin with foil. Spoon mixture in, and smooth it out. Freeze overnight.**

3 Turn foil and ice cream out onto a plate and peel off foil.

4 Return the cake to the freezer until ready to serve. Decorate with extra fruit, flowers, and candles.

Drinks

Try not to drink soda, even at a party. Soda contains **acid**. Acid weakens the hard enamel covering of your teeth. The best drink is water.

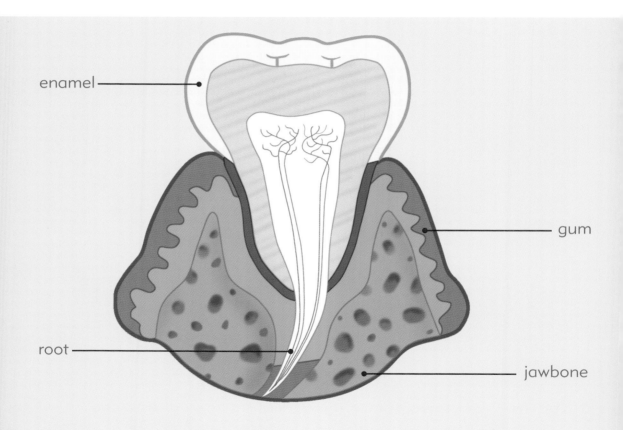

enamel

gum

root

jawbone

Weak tooth enamel can lead to holes in your teeth.

You could decorate water bottles to match the party theme. Water helps clean your teeth after eating party food.

Decorated bottles make drinking water look scary.

Make party punch

You can serve this healthy fizzy **punch** in large jugs. You do not need a punchbowl.

What you need
- 1½ gallons (7 liters) orange juice (unsweetened)
- 16 ounces (500 milliliters) pineapple juice (unsweetened)
- 28 ounces (1 liter) sparkling mineral water
- ice

What to do
1 **Mix the orange juice and pineapple juice together.**
2 **Place in the fridge to cool.**
3 **Add mineral water and ice just before serving.**
4 **Serve and enjoy!**

Make ice-block surprises

Ask a parent or teacher for help.

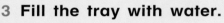

Add these healthy ice-block surprises to party punch or jugs of water.

What you need
- water
- strawberries, grapes, kiwi, watermelon, or another favorite fruit
- ice-block tray

What to do
1 **Slice the fruit into small pieces.**
2 **Place a fruit piece into each section of an ice-block tray.**
3 **Fill the tray with water.**
4 **Freeze overnight.**

Party bags

When the party is over, it is nice to give each of your guests something. Try to think of small gifts that match your party theme.

This scary party bag is full of fun, not sugar.

Instead of party bags, your guests could each make a craft item to take home. These ideas may help you.

painted glass jar

decorated pillow case

A craft store will have special paints for glass, and felt-tip fabric pens.

Healthy choices for life

Making healthy choices in everything you do will help you to be fit, happy, and healthy.

Life is fun when you make healthy choices.

Glossary

acid   a chemical substance that can eat away tooth enamel

balance   an equal amount of different things

decorate   to make something look more beautiful

energy   strength to do things

nutrients   healthy substances found in food, such as vitamins and minerals

punch   a drink made with water, juice, ice, and sometimes, pieces of fruit

sugary   containing a lot of sugar

Index

b
birthday cake   22–23

c
chicken nuggets   16–17
crafts   29

d
dip   10
dippers   11

f
fat group   5
food group pyramid   4, 5
fruit and vegetable group   5
fruit plate   9
fruit sticks   21

g
games   7
grain group   5

i
ice   25
ice-block surprises   27

m
meat group   5
milk group   5

n
nibbles   8

p
party bags   28
punch   26

r
recipes   10, 11, 14–15, 16–17,
        18–19, 21, 22–23, 26, 27

s
sandwiches   12
soft drinks   24
sugar   6
sugar group   5
sweet treats   20

t
teeth   24
theme   13, 25, 28

w
water   4, 24, 25